Winter Warmers

50 of the Healthiest Slow Cooker Recipes

Disclaimer

Copyright © September 2014 Winter Warmers, Healthy Crock Pot Recipes by Sophie Miller. All rights reserved. No part of this publication may be reproduced, distributed, or transmitted in any form or by any means, including photocopying, recording, or other electronic or mechanical methods, without the prior written permission of the publisher, except in the case of brief quotations embodied in critical reviews and certain other noncommercial uses permitted by copyright law. For permission requests, write to the publisher, addressed "Attention: Permissions Coordinator".

Although the author and publisher have made every effort to ensure that the information in this book was correct at press time, the author and publisher do not assume and hereby disclaim any liability to any party for any loss, injury, damage or disruption caused by errors or omissions, whether such errors or omissions result from negligence, accident, non-functional websites, or any other cause. Any advice or strategy contained herein may not be suitable for every individual.

Contents

Introduction to Slow Cooking 6
Benefits of Slow Cooking 7
Healthy Alternatives for Cooking Fats 9
Healthy Slow Cooker Recipes 11
   Breakfast Recipes 12
      Banana Walnut Bread 13
      Ham and Cheese Egg Casserole 15
      Caramel Apple French Toast Casserole 16
      Blueberry Walnut Porridge 18
      Chicken Sausage Breakfast Casserole 19
      Crustless Spinach Mushroom Quiche 21
      Pumpkin Quinoa Porridge 22
      Overnight Raisin Cinnamon Oatmeal 24
      Mexican Breakfast Casserole 25
      Blueberry Maple French Toast Casserole 27
   Lunch Recipes 29
      Tuscan Chicken Soup 30
      Pulled Pork Sandwiches 32
      Cheesy Enchilada Stack 34
      Buffalo Chicken Drumsticks 36
      Caribbean Black Bean Soup 38
      Turkey with Asian Vegetables 40
      Rosemary Pork Sliders with Spicy Mustard 42
      Potato Leek Soup 44
      Chilaquiles 46
      Vegetarian Pot Pie 48
   Dinner Recipes 50
      Char Siu Pork Roast 52

Beef Brisket with Stout 54

Smoky Chili 56

Osso Buco 58

Pork and Vegetable Curry 60

Chicken Chasseur 62

Smoky Sausage Cassoulet 64

Beef Stroganoff 66

Chicken Provencal 68

Satsuma Turkey with Steamed Rice 70

Meatballs in Spicy, Chunky Tomato Ragu 72

Chinese Beef and Noodles 74

Tunisian-Style Lamb with Pumpkin Couscous 76

Rosemary Lamb Shanks 78

Chicken and Broccoli Bake 80

Chicken and Chorizo Jambalaya 81

Chicken Cacciatore 83

Five-Spice Caramel Pork (Thit Heo Kho Tieu) 85

Shepherd's Pie 87

Meatloaf 89

Sweet Treat Recipes 91

Almond Apple Streusel 92

Spiced Pumpkin Pie Pudding 94

Walnut-Stuffed Apples 96

Triple Berry Cobbler 97

Peach Caramel Pudding 99

Fudgy Chocolate Cola Cake 101

Cinnamon Rice Pudding 103

Poached Pears with Balsamic Vinegar 105

Pineapple Bananas Foster 107

Tropical Coconut Tapioca Pudding 108

Conclusion 110

About the Author 111

Introduction to Slow Cooking

  If you have made the commitment to following a healthy diet you may now be facing the challenge of coming up with meals to prepare on a daily basis. You can only eat so many salads or grilled chicken breasts before you become bored and are tempted to break your diet for the convenience of fast food. If you are facing this type of struggle, fear not – an easy solution exists. The slow cooker (also known as a Crockpot) is an electric kitchen appliance that enables you to cook foods at low temperature over long periods of time, leaving you free to do the things you need to do. Most slow cooker recipes require only a few minutes of preparation time, then you simply turn it on and let it cook! When you come home a hot and delicious meal will be ready and waiting for you and your family to enjoy.

  In this book you will discover the basics about slow cooking and receive a collection of delicious slow cooker recipes. First you will receive an overview of the many benefits associated with slow cooking. As you will see, slow cooking is a great method to employ when you want to prepare a healthy meal for your family but do not have a lot of extra time on your hands. You will also receive tips for substituting healthier cooking oils in your recipes so you can stick to your commitment to better health. Finally, you will receive a collection of 50 delicious (and healthy!) slow-cooker recipes for breakfast, lunch, dinner, and dessert.

Benefits of Slow Cooking

After receiving some basic information about what slow cooking is, you may be wondering why you should consider incorporating it into your routine. Below you will find a list of the many benefits associated with slow cooking:

1. Long cooking times allows complex flavors to develop and be better distributed throughout the ingredients

2. Low cooking temperature over long periods of time renders tough and inexpensive cuts of meat tender and delicious

3. There is little to no risk of burning food – spraying the slow cooker will prevent any from sticking to the bottom as well

4. Using a slow cooker means that your oven and stove are left open for other uses – this is particularly useful during the holidays

5. Many slow cooker recipes take most of the day to prepare which means that you can "set it and forget it"

6. Using a slow cooker enables you to spend only a few minutes preparing a meal that will be fully cooked and ready to enjoy a few hours later – with

not extra effort on your part

7. Slow cooking is a very versatile cooking method – it can be applied to soups, stews, side dishes, entrees and even desserts

Healthy Alternatives for Cooking Fats

When it comes to preparing healthy meals for your family, the items you exclude from your recipes are just as important as the items you include. Using plenty of fresh vegetables, lean meats and spices are great but if you continue to use unhealthy cooking fats like butter and margarine, your meals will not be as healthy as you think they are. Below you will find an overview of some of the best cooking oils to use when preparing your healthy slow cooker dishes:

1. **Olive Oil** – This type of oil is one of the most popular for cooking because it is versatile and healthy. Cold-pressed olive oil is the best way to go because it has not been chemically hydrogenated or altered like many vegetable oils are. Olive oil is an excellent source of monounsaturated fat as well as antioxidants called polyphenols which have been linked to cardiac benefits.

2. **Coconut Oil** – This particular oil is widely regarded as one of the healthiest options available when it comes to cooking oil. Unlike olive oil, coconut oil is actually solid at room temperature so, if you want to use it for baking, you may need to melt it first. Coconut oil contains 92% saturated fat, 6% monounsaturated fat, and 2% polyunsaturated fat – all of

these fats are considered to be heart-healthy and good for you. Coconut oil also boosts your metabolism, helping your body to burn more fat.

3. **Avocado Oil** – In many ways, avocado oil is similar to olive oil – it can be cold-pressed and it is rich in monounsaturated fats. Avocado oil contains phytosterols which have been shown to help reduce bad cholesterol (LDL) levels as well as vitamin E which may help to improve overall cardiac health.

Healthy Slow Cooker Recipes

If you are unfamiliar with slow cooking, this book is the perfect place to start. Here you will find a collection of 50 different slow cooker recipes made with healthy and flavorful ingredients. Below you will find a list of the categories of recipes provided in this book.

Recipe Categories in this Book:

Breakfast Recipes

Lunch Recipes

Dinner Recipes

Sweet Treat Recipes

Breakfast Recipes

Recipes Included in this Section:

Banana Walnut Bread

Ham and Cheese Egg Casserole

Caramel Apple French Toast Casserole

Blueberry Walnut Porridge

Chicken Sausage Breakfast Casserole

Crustless Spinach Mushroom Quiche

Pumpkin Quinoa Porridge

Overnight Apple Cinnamon Oatmeal

Mexican Breakfast Casserole

Blueberry Maple French Toast Casserole

Banana Walnut Bread

Servings: 4

Ingredients:

½ cup plus 2 tablespoons all-purpose flour

¼ teaspoon baking soda

1/8 teaspoon salt

3 tablespoons coconut oil, melted

¼ cup light brown sugar, packed

1 large egg, whisked

1 tablespoon skim milk

¾ teaspoon vanilla extract

1 large banana, mashed

3 to 4 tablespoons chopped walnuts

Instructions:

1. Lightly grease a mini loaf pan and place it in the slow cooker on top of a ring of foil to keep it off the bottom.
2. Combine the flour, baking soda and salt in a mixing bowl.

Banana Walnut Bread

3. In a separate bowl, beat together the coconut oil, brown sugar, egg, milk and vanilla – fold in the mashed banana.
4. Stir the dry ingredients into the wet then fold in the walnuts.
5. Spoon the batter into the prepared pan.
6. Cover and cook on high heat for 2 hours until a knife inserted in the center comes out clean.
7. Remove the loaf pan from the slow cooker and turn the loaf out onto a wire rack to cool.

Ham and Cheese Egg Casserole

Servings: 6

Ingredients:

6 large eggs, whisked

¼ cup fat-free milk

½ cup plain Greek yogurt

½ teaspoon salt

¼ teaspoon black pepper

1 cup diced deli ham (fat-free)

1 cup reduced-fat shredded cheddar cheese

3 green onions, sliced thin

Instructions:

1. Lightly grease the insert of your slow cooker with cooking spray.
2. Whisk together the eggs, milk, yogurt, salt and pepper in a mixing bowl.
3. Fold in the ham, cheese and green onions.
4. Pour the mixture into the slow cooker then cover and cook on high heat for 1 ½ to 2 hours until the center is set.

Caramel Apple French Toast Casserole

Servings: 8

Ingredients:

8 large eggs, whisked

2 cups half-and-half

½ cup fat-free milk

1 1/3 cup light brown sugar, packed and divided

1 ¼ teaspoons vanilla extract

1 ½ teaspoons ground cinnamon, divided

10 cups cubed French bread

½ cup coconut oil, melted and divided

3 medium apples, peeled, cored and chopped

1 cup chopped pecans

Instructions:

1. Lightly grease the insert of your slow cooker with cooking spray.
2. Beat the eggs, half-and-half, milk, 1/3 cup brown sugar, vanilla extract and ¾ teaspoon cinnamon in a mixing bowl.
3. Fold in the cubed bread and let it stand for 15 minutes to absorb the liquid.

Caramel Apple French Toast Casserole

4. Meanwhile, heat 2 tablespoons coconut oil in a small skillet over medium heat.
5. Add the apples and cook for 5 minutes until tender.
6. Whisk together the remaining coconut oil, brown sugar, cinnamon and pecans in a mixing bowl.
7. Spoon half the bread mixture into the slow cooker and top with half the apples and half of the brown sugar pecan mixture.
8. Repeat the layers then cover and cook on low heat for 2 ½ to 3 hours until the center is set.

Blueberry Walnut Porridge

Servings: 8

Ingredients:

3 ½ cups fat-free milk

3 ½ cups water

2 cups 8-grain hot cereal blend

2 cups fresh blueberries

½ teaspoon ground cinnamon

½ teaspoon salt

1/3 cup raw honey

1/3 cup toasted walnuts, chopped

Instructions:

1. Lightly grease the insert of your slow cooker with cooking spray.
2. Stir together the milk, water and 8-grain cereal blend in the slow cooker.
3. Add ½ cup blueberries along with the cinnamon and salt.
4. Cover and cook on low heat for 8 to 9 hours.
5. Stir in the remaining blueberries along with the honey in the morning.
6. Spoon the porridge into bowls and sprinkle with walnuts to serve.

Chicken Sausage Breakfast Casserole

Servings: 8

Ingredients:

1 (32 ounce) bag frozen hash brown potatoes

1 lbs. cooked chicken sausage links, chopped

1 small yellow onion, diced

1 ½ cups reduced-fat shredded cheddar cheese

1 small green pepper, cored and diced

12 large eggs, whisked

1 cup fat-free milk

Instructions:

1. Lightly grease the insert of your slow cooker with cooking spray.
2. Combine the onion, green pepper and ½ cup shredded cheddar in a bowl. Stir well.
3. Spread half of the frozen hash browns on the bottom of the slow cooker and sprinkle half the chicken sausage over top.
4. Spoon half of the onion mixture over the chicken sausage and top with another layer of hash browns.
5. Sprinkle on the remaining chicken sausage along with the rest of the onion mixture.

6. Top the casserole with the remaining cheese.
7. Whisk together the eggs and milk then pour into the slow cooker.
8. Cover and cook on low heat for 4 to 5 hours until the center is set.

Crustless Spinach Mushroom Quiche

Servings: 8

Ingredients:

8 large eggs, whisked

1 cup fat-free milk

1 cup baking mix

2 cups baby spinach, packed

1 ½ cups diced mushrooms

½ cup sweet red pepper, diced

2 tablespoons fresh chopped basil

1 clove minced garlic

Instructions:

1. Lightly grease the insert of your slow cooker with cooking spray.
2. Beat together the eggs, milk and baking mix in a mixing bowl until thoroughly combined.
3. Fold in the spinach, mushrooms, red peppers, basil and garlic.
4. Spoon the mixture into the slow cooker then cover and cook on high heat for 3 to 4 hours or on low for 5 to 6 hours until the center is set.
5. Remove the quiche from the slow cooker and cut into wedges to serve.

Pumpkin Quinoa Porridge

Servings: 6

Ingredients:

4 pitted dates, chopped

3 cups unsweetened almond milk (or skim milk)

1 cup uncooked quinoa, rinsed well

1 medium ripe apple, cored and diced

1 ½ teaspoon ground cinnamon

1 teaspoon vanilla extract

¼ teaspoon ground nutmeg

Pinch salt

Toasted pumpkin seeds

Instructions:

1. Lightly grease the insert of your slow cooker with cooking spray.
2. Combine all of the ingredients in the slow cooker and stir well.
3. Cover and cook on low heat for 6 to 8 hours (or overnight) until hot and thick.
4. Sprinkle with toasted pumpkin seed to serve.

Pumpkin Quinoa Porridge

Overnight Raisin Cinnamon Oatmeal

Servings: 8

Ingredients:

2 medium ripe apples, cored and diced

1 ½ cups unsweetened coconut milk

1 ½ cups water

1 cup steel-cut oats

2 tablespoons light brown sugar, packed

1 tablespoon coconut oil

¾ teaspoon ground cinnamon

Pinch salt

Instructions:

1. Lightly grease the insert of your slow cooker with cooking spray.
2. Combine all ingredients but the raisins in the slow cooker and stir well.
3. Cover and cook on low heat for 6 to 7 hours until the oats are tender.
4. Spoon the oatmeal into bowls and top with raisins to serve.

Mexican Breakfast Casserole

Servings: 8

Ingredients:

9 small corn tortillas

8 large eggs, whisked

1 ½ cups fat-free milk

1 jalapeno pepper, seeded and minced

1 lbs. lean ground beef, cooked and crumbled

2 cups reduced-fat shredded Mexican cheese

Instructions:

1. Lightly grease the insert of your slow cooker with cooking spray.
2. Line the bottom of the slow cooker with 3 tortillas, cutting them as needed to fit.
3. Whisk together the eggs, milk and jalapeno in a mixing bowl.
4. Set aside 2 tablespoons each of diced red pepper and green onion.
5. Spread half the ground beef over the tortillas and top with half the remaining red pepper and green onions.
6. Sprinkle with ¾ cups shredded Mexican cheese then top with another 3 tortillas.

7. Repeat the layers, using the second half of the ground beef, red pepper and green onions.
8. Top the second layer of red pepper and green onions with ¾ cup cheese and the final 3 tortillas.
9. Pour the egg mixture into the slow cooker then sprinkle with the remaining ½ cup cheese.
10. Cover and cook on low heat for 4 to 5 hours until the center is set.
11. Sprinkle with the reserved red pepper and green onions to serve.

Blueberry Maple French Toast Casserole

Servings: 8

Ingredients:

2 large eggs plus 2 whites, whisked

1 ½ cups fat-free milk

2 tablespoons honey

1 ¼ teaspoon vanilla extract

¼ teaspoon ground cinnamon

10 slices whole-grain bread

For the Filling:

3 cups fresh blueberries

3 tablespoons maple syrup

1 teaspoon fresh lemon juice

1 teaspoon ground cinnamon

¼ cup chopped pecans

Instructions:

1. Lightly grease the insert of your slow cooker with cooking spray.
2. Whisk together the eggs, egg whites, milk, honey, vanilla and cinnamon in a mixing bowl.
3. To prepare the filling, combine the maple syrup, lemon juice, pecans and cinnamon in a separate mixing bowl.
4. Stir in the blueberries and set aside.
5. Slice the bread into triangles and arrange one layer in the bottom of the slow cooker.
6. Spoon about ¼ of the blueberry filling over the bread then repeat the layers, ending with the last of the filling on top.
7. Pour the egg mixture into the slow cooker then cover and cook on high heat for 2 to 2 ½ hours or on low heat for 4 hours until the center is set.

Lunch Recipes

Recipes Included in this Section:

Tuscan Chicken Soup

Pulled Pork Sandwiches

Cheesy Enchilada Stack

Buffalo Chicken Drumsticks

Caribbean Black Bean Soup

Turkey with Asian Vegetables

Rosemary Pork Sliders with Spicy Mustard

Potato Leek Soup

Chilaquiles

Vegetarian Pot Pie

Tuscan Chicken Soup

Servings: 6

Ingredients:

1 lbs. boneless skinless chicken breast, chopped

1 small yellow onion, diced

1 (15 ounce) can white cannellini beans, rinsed and drained

1 (14 ounce) can chicken broth

1 small bottle roasted red peppers, drained and chopped

2 tablespoons tomato paste

1 tablespoon minced garlic

Salt and pepper to taste

6 ounces fresh baby spinach

1 sprig fresh rosemary

Parmesan cheese to serve

Instructions:

1. Combine all of the ingredients except for the spinach and rosemary in the slow cooker.
2. Stir well then cover and cook on high heat for 1 hour.

3. Reduce the heat to low then cook for another 3 hours until the vegetables are tender.
4. Stir in the spinach and rosemary then cook, covered, for another 10 minutes on low heat.
5. Spoon the soup onto bowls and serve hot with parmesan cheese.

Pulled Pork Sandwiches

Servings: 12

Ingredients:

3 lbs. boneless pork loin, fat trimmed

1 cup water

2 cups barbecue sauce

2 tablespoons light brown sugar, packed

1 teaspoon fresh ground pepper

Toasted sandwich buns

Coleslaw, optional

Instructions:

1. Place the pork shoulder in the center of the slow cooker and pour the water over it.
2. Cover and cook on low heat for 7 hours until the pork is very tender.
3. Remove the pork from the slow cooker and discard the cooking liquid.
4. Shred the pork with two forks and return it to the slow cooker.
5. Stir in the barbecue sauce, brown sugar and pepper.
6. Cover and cook on low heat for 1 hour until hot.

7. Serve the pulled pork hot on toasted sandwich buns topped with fresh coleslaw, if desired.

Cheesy Enchilada Stack

Servings: 8

Ingredients:

½ lbs. lean ground turkey breast

1 ½ teaspoon minced garlic

1 small poblano chile, seeded and diced

1 cup diced yellow onion

1 (14.5 ounce) can diced tomatoes

2 teaspoons chipotle chile powder

1 cup tomato sauce

1 cup frozen corn kernels

1 (15 ounce) can black beans, rinsed and drained

5 (8-inch) whole wheat flour tortillas

1 ½ cups reduced-fat shredded cheddar cheese

Instructions:

1. Heat the ground turkey in a large skillet over medium-high heat.
2. Stir in the garlic and chiles and cook until the turkey is evenly browned.
3. Remove the turkey to a bowl and reheat the skillet over medium-high heat.

4. Add the onions and tomatoes – cook for 4 to 5 minutes until the onion is translucent.
5. Stir in the chili powder and tomato sauce then spoon the mixture into a blender and blend until smooth.
6. Lightly grease the slow cooker with cooking spray then spoon 4 tablespoons of the tomato sauce into it.
7. In a large bowl, stir together the cooked turkey, tomato sauce, corn and beans.
8. Place one tortilla in the center of the slow cooker and top with 1 cup of the ground turkey mixture and sprinkle with ¼ cup cheese.
9. Repeat the layers of tortilla, turkey mixture and cheese until you run out.
10. Cover the slow cooker and cook on low heat for 2 hours until the cheese is melted and the filling hot.
11. Cut into wedges to serve.

Buffalo Chicken Drumsticks

Servings: 8 to 10

Ingredients:

3 lbs. raw chicken drumsticks

Salt and pepper to taste

1 cup hot sauce

2 ½ tablespoons apple cider vinegar

1 teaspoon Worcestershire sauce

2 teaspoons minced garlic

Instructions:

1. Preheat the oven to 450°F and line a baking sheet with foil.
2. Arrange the chicken on the baking sheet and coat with cooking spray.
3. Season lightly with salt and pepper to taste then bake for 8 to 10 minutes until lightly browned.
4. Whisk together the hot sauce, cider vinegar, Worcestershire sauce and garlic in a small bowl.
5. Pour the sauce into the slow cooker then add the chicken, tossing gently.
6. Cover and cook on high heat for 3 to 4 hours until the chicken legs are cooked through.

7. Serve with ranch or blue cheese dressing for dipping.

Caribbean Black Bean Soup

Servings: 8

Ingredients:

1 large red onion, chopped

1 small red pepper, cored and diced

1 small green pepper, cored and diced

2 small jalapeno peppers, seeded and minced

¼ cup tomato paste

4 cups vegetable broth

1 ¼ teaspoons dried thyme

¾ teaspoon ground cumin

½ teaspoon fresh ground pepper

¼ teaspoon cayenne pepper

2 (15 ounce) can black beans, rinsed and drained

½ cup canned coconut milk

½ bunch fresh chopped cilantro

2 limes, cut into wedges

Instructions:

1. Combine all of the ingredients aside from the coconut milk, cilantro and lime wedges in the slow cooker.
2. Stir well then cover and cook on low heat for 8 hours.
3. Whisk in the coconut milk then spoon the soup into bowls.
4. Garnish with fresh cilantro and lime wedges to serve.

Turkey with Asian Vegetables

Servings: 8

Ingredients:

8 ounces sliced crimini mushrooms

1 medium red pepper, sliced thin

4 baby bok choy, quartered

1 can baby corn, drained

1 can bamboo shoots, drained

2 ½ tablespoons hoisin sauce

1 ½ tablespoons oyster sauce

1 tablespoon reduced-sodium soy sauce

1 tablespoon fresh minced ginger

1 tablespoon minced garlic

1 tablespoon olive oil

4 lbs. bone-in turkey drumsticks, skin removed

1 teaspoon Chinese five-spice powder

2 cups thinly sliced Chinese cabbage

½ cup fresh chopped cilantro

¼ cup sliced green onion

Instructions:

1. Combine the mushrooms, peppers, bok choy, baby corn and bamboo shoots in the slow cooker.
2. Whisk together the hoisin, oyster sauce, soy sauce, ginger, and garlic in a small bowl.
3. Stir the sauce into the slow cooker.
4. Heat the oil in a large skillet over medium-high heat.
5. Add the turkey and sprinkle with five-spice powder and cook for 2 to 3 minutes on each side until browned.
6. Transfer the turkey to the slow cooker then cover and cook on low heat for 5 to 6 hours until the turkey is tender.
7. Remove the turkey to a cutting board and remove the bones – chop the flesh.
8. Stir the chopped turkey back into the slow cooker then stir in the cabbage.
9. Sprinkle with cilantro and green onions to serve.

Rosemary Pork Sliders with Spicy Mustard

Servings: 10 to 12

Ingredients:

1 tablespoon olive oil

1 (1 ½ lbs.) boneless pork loin, trimmed

Fresh ground pepper

1 cup water

1 cup chicken broth

1 small yellow onion, chopped

1 tablespoon fresh chopped rosemary

1 tablespoon minced garlic

Whole-wheat sandwich buns

Spicy whole-grain mustard

Instructions:

1. Heat the oil in a large skillet over medium-high heat.
2. Season the pork with pepper then add to the skillet.
3. Cook for 2 to 3 minutes on each side until browned then transfer to the slow cooker.

4. Stir together the water, chicken broth, onions, rosemary and garlic then pour into the slow cooker.
5. Cover and cook on low heat for 8 hours until the pork is tender.
6. Remove the pork to a cutting board and shred with two forks.
7. Strain the cooking liquid through a mesh sieve and discard the solids.
8. Return the pork to the slow cooker with 1 cup of the cooking liquid.
9. Serve the pork hot on top of toasted whole-wheat sandwich buns with spicy mustard.

Potato Leek Soup

Servings: 8

Ingredients:

3 slices uncooked bacon

3 lbs. baking potatoes, peeled and sliced

1 large leek, chopped (light green and white parts only)

1 small yellow onion, diced

½ cup water

2 (15 ounce) cans chicken broth

2 cups fat-free milk

Salt and pepper to taste

1 cup reduced-fat shredded cheddar cheese

Instructions:

1. Heat the bacon in a large skillet over medium-high heat until crisp.
2. Remove the bacon to paper towels to drain then coarsely chop.
3. Combine the potato, leeks and onion in the slow cooker.
4. Stir in the water, chicken broth and milk – season lightly with salt and pepper to taste.
5. Cover and cook on low heat for 8 hours until the potatoes are very tender.

6. Use a potato masher to mash the mixture in the slow cooker then stir in the milk and ¾ cup cheese.
7. Increase the heat to high and cook, covered, for 20 minutes.
8. Spoon the soup into bowls and garnish with chopped bacon and the remaining cheese to serve.

Chilaquiles

Servings: 8 to 10

Ingredients:

1 tablespoon olive oil

2 ½ lbs. bone-in chicken thighs or breasts

1 large red onion, chopped

1 medium red bell pepper, cored and chopped

1 medium green bell pepper, cored and chopped

1 cup chicken broth

¼ cup fresh chopped cilantro

3 teaspoons ground cumin

2 tablespoons minced garlic

2 (28 ounce) cans diced tomatoes

1 small can green chiles, chopped

Tortilla chips

Instructions:

1. Heat the oil in a large skillet over medium-high heat.

2. Add the chicken and cook for 2 to 3 minutes on each side until lightly browned.
3. Combine the onion, bell peppers, chicken broth, cilantro, cumin, garlic, tomatoes and chiles in the slow cooker.
4. Transfer the chicken to the slow cooker on top of the other ingredients.
5. Cover and cook on low heat for 4 hours until the chicken is cooked through.
6. Remove the chicken with a slotted spoon and cut out the bones.
7. Return the chicken to the slow cooker, stir well, and then serve the soup ladled over tortilla chips.

Vegetarian Pot Pie

Servings: 8

Ingredients:

1 tablespoon olive oil

2 cups Yukon gold potato, diced

3 medium carrots, peeled and chopped

3 medium stalks celery, sliced

1 large yellow onion, diced

2 (8-ounce) packages sliced mushrooms

1 teaspoon minced garlic

Salt and pepper to taste

For the Topping:

1 2/3 cups all-purpose flour

1 ¾ teaspoons baking powder

½ teaspoon baking soda

1 teaspoon black pepper

Pinch salt

¼ cup unsalted butter, chopped

1/3 cup fresh grated parmesan cheese

1 cup low-fat buttermilk

Instructions:

1. Lightly grease a slow cooker with cooking spray.
2. Combine the olive oil, potato, carrot, celery, onion, mushrooms, garlic, salt and pepper in the slow cooker.
3. In a small saucepan over medium-high heat, melt the coconut oil.
4. Whisk in the flour and cook for 1 minute, stirring constantly.
5. Pour in the milk in a steady stream while whisking then whisk in the vegetable broth.
6. Cook for 2 to 3 minutes until hot and bubbling then pour into the slow cooker.
7. Stir in the peas and rosemary then cover and cook on low heat for 3 ½ hours.
8. To prepare the topping, stir together the flour, baking powder, baking soda, salt and pepper in a mixing bowl.
9. Cut in the butter to form a crumbled mixture then stir in the cheese and buttermilk until just moistened.
10. Drop the mixture into the slow cooker into 7 to 9 mounds.
11. Increase the heat to high and cook, covered, for 1 hour 15 minutes until the biscuits are cooked through.
12. Let stand, uncovered, for 5 minutes before serving.

Dinner Recipes

Recipes Included in this Section:

Char Siu Pork Roast

Beef Brisket with Stout

Smoky Chili

Osso Buco

Pork and Vegetable Curry

Chicken Chasseur

Smoky Sausage Cassoulet

Beef Stroganoff

Chicken Provencal

Satsuma Turkey with Steamed Rice

Meatballs in Spicy, Chunky Tomato Ragu

Chinese Beef and Noodles

Tunisian-Style Lamb with Couscous

Rosemary Lamb Shanks

Chicken and Broccoli Bake

Chicken and Chorizo Jambalaya

Chicken Cacciatore

Five-Spice Caramel Pork

Shepherd's Pie

Meatloaf

Char Siu Pork Roast

Servings: 8

Ingredients:

5 tablespoons reduced-sodium soy sauce

3 tablespoons hoisin sauce

3 tablespoons ketchup

2 ½ tablespoons honey

1 tablespoon minced garlic

2 teaspoons fresh minced ginger

¾ teaspoon toasted sesame oil

½ teaspoon Chinese five-spice powder

2 lbs. boneless pork shoulder, trimmed

½ cup chicken broth

Instructions:

1. Stir together the soy sauce, hoisin, ketchup, honey, garlic, ginger, sesame oil and Chinese five-spice powder in a small bowl.
2. Place the pork in a plastic freezer bag and pour in the sauce.

3. Shake to coat then marinate in the refrigerator for at least 2 hours, turning over occasionally to evenly coat.
4. Transfer the pork and sauce to the slow cooker.
5. Cover and cook on low heat for 8 hours until the pork is tender.
6. Remove the pork to a cutting board and cover with foil.
7. Whisk the broth into the slow cooker then cook, covered, for 30 minutes until thickened.
8. Meanwhile, shred the pork with two forks and stir it back into the slow cooker.
9. Serve the pork hot on corn tortillas or over steamed brown rice.

Beef Brisket with Stout

Servings: 6-8

Ingredients:

3 lbs. beef brisket, fat trimmed

1 tablespoon olive oil

¼ cup water

1 large yellow onion, chopped

1 ½ cups sliced carrot

1 (12 ounce) bottle stout beer

1 tablespoon balsamic vinegar

Instructions:

1. Season the brisket with salt and pepper to taste.
2. Heat the oil in a large skillet over medium-high heat and add the brisket.
3. Cook for 2 to 3 minutes on each side until browned – about 10 minutes total.
4. Pour ¼ cup water into the pan and cook to loosen bits of browned meat then stir in the onion and carrots.
5. Cook for 5 minutes until the vegetables are tender then transfer to the slow cooker.
6. Place the brisket on top of the vegetables in the slow cooker.

7. Pour in the vinegar and stout beer.
8. Cover and cook for 8 hours on low heat until the brisket is tender.
9. Slice the brisket across the grain and serve with the sauce over whole-wheat pasta or mashed potatoes.

Smoky Chili

Servings: 8

Ingredients:

2 lbs. ground pork

2 large yellow onions, chopped

2 medium green peppers, cored and chopped

1 tablespoon minced garlic

3 tablespoons tomato paste

1 cup lager beer

2 ½ tablespoons chili powder

1 tablespoon ground cumin

1 ½ teaspoons dried oregano

½ teaspoon black pepper

3 (14.5 ounce) cans diced tomatoes

1 (15 ounce) can pinto beans, rinsed and drained

1 cup tomato sauce

½ lbs. smoked ham, diced

2 tablespoons honey

½ cup fresh chopped cilantro

4 green onions, sliced thin

Instructions:

1. Heat the ground pork in skillet over medium heat until lightly browned.
2. Transfer the pork to the slow cooker and stir in the onion, bell pepper, garlic and tomato paste.
3. Stir in the beer, chili powder, cumin, oregano, pepper, tomatoes, beans, tomato sauce, smoked ham, and bay leaf.
4. Cover and cook on high heat for 5 hours then discard the bay leaf.
5. Stir in the honey then spoon into bowls to serve.
6. Garnish with fresh chopped cilantro and green onions.

Osso Buco

Servings: 8

Ingredients:

2/3 cup all-purpose flour

½ teaspoon salt

¼ teaspoon black pepper

5 lbs. veal shanks, fat trimmed

2 cups chopped red onion

1 ¼ cups sliced celery

2 tablespoons minced garlic

4 cups low-sodium beef broth

2 cups dry white wine

2 teaspoons dried rosemary

Instructions:

1. Combine the flour, salt and pepper then toss with the veal shanks until coated.
2. Heat the oil in a large skillet over medium heat.

3. Add the veal and cook for 2 to 3 minutes on each side until browned then transfer to the slow cooker.
4. Add the onion, celery and garlic.
5. Stir together the broth, wine and rosemary then pour into the slow cooker.
6. Cover and cook on low heat for 8 to 9 hours until the veal is cooked through.
7. Serve hot over cooked whole-wheat pasta with the sauce from the slow cooker.

Pork and Vegetable Curry

Servings:

Ingredients:

1 tablespoon olive oil

2 lbs. boneless pork, sliced thin

1 large yellow onion, sliced

1 tablespoon minced garlic

1 cup chicken broth

1 tablespoon brown sugar, packed

3 tablespoons green curry paste

2 tablespoons fish sauce

1 ½ tablespoons fresh lime juice

1 (14 ounce) can light coconut milk

1 jalapeno pepper, seeded and minced

2 cups baby spinach leaves

1 cup chopped broccoli florets

3 green onions, cut into 2-inch chunks

Fresh chopped cilantro

Instructions:

1. Heat the oil in a skillet over medium heat.
2. Add the pork and cook for 5 minutes, stirring occasionally, until evenly browned.
3. Transfer the pork to the slow cooker.
4. Stir in the onion and garlic.
5. In a mixing bowl, whisk together the chicken broth, brown sugar, curry paste, fish sauce, lime juice and coconut milk.
6. Stir the mixture into the slow cooker along with the jalapeno pepper.
7. Cover and cook on low heat for 6 hours.
8. Stir in the spinach, broccoli and green onion then cook for another 30 minutes on low heat until the vegetables are tender.
9. Spoon into bowls and serve garnished with fresh chopped cilantro.

Chicken Chasseur

Servings: 6

Ingredients:

6 slices turkey bacon, uncooked

12 bone-in chicken thighs

1 lbs. sliced crimini mushrooms

1 medium red onion, chopped

1 tablespoon minced garlic

1 ½ cups dry white wine

2 tablespoons tomato paste

1 (14.5 ounce) can diced tomatoes

2 cups chicken broth

1 teaspoon dried thyme

2 bay leaves

¼ cup all-purpose flour

½ cup water

Instructions:

1. Heat the turkey bacon in a large skillet over medium-high heat until crisp.
2. Drain the bacon on paper towel then chop coarsely.
3. Reheat the skillet to medium-high heat and add the chicken – cook for 2 to 3 minutes on each side until browned.
4. Transfer the chicken to the slow cooker and top with the onions, mushrooms and garlic.
5. Stir in the wine, tomato paste, tomatoes, broth, bay leaf and thyme.
6. Cover and cook on low heat for 4 hours until the chicken is cooked through.
7. Remove the chicken to a serving platter and discard the bay leaf.
8. Whisk together the flour and water then stir into the slow cooker.
9. Cover and cook on high for another 20 to 30 minutes until the sauce is thick.
10. Serve the chicken hot with the sauce and vegetables.

Smoky Sausage Cassoulet

Servings: 8

Ingredients:

3 slices turkey bacon, uncooked

1 large yellow onion, chopped

1 tablespoon minced garlic

1 teaspoon dried rosemary

½ teaspoon dried thyme

2 (15 ounce) cans diced tomatoes

½ teaspoon black pepper

2 (15 ounce) cans white beans, rinsed and drained

1 lbs. lean boneless pork, chopped

½ lbs. smoked pork sausage, chopped

Instructions:

1. Heat the turkey bacon in a large skillet over medium-high heat until crisp.
2. Drain the bacon on paper towel then chop coarsely.
3. Add the onion and garlic to the skillet and cook for 3 minutes, stirring often.

4. Transfer the onion mixture to the slow cooker and stir in the rosemary, thyme along with the bacon, tomatoes and pepper.
5. Mash half of the beans in bowl with a potato masher then stir in the remaining beans along with the chopped pork and sausage.
6. Spoon half of the bean mixture into the slow cooker then top with the onion and tomato mixture.
7. Top with the remaining bean mixture then cover and cook on low heat for 5 hours.
8. Spoon into bowls to serve.

Healthy Slow Cooker Reipes

Ingredients:

1 lbs. sirloin beef, cut into chunks

1 medium yellow onion, chopped

2 ounces sliced mushrooms

1 tablespoon minced garlic

3 tablespoons fresh chopped parsley

1 ½ tablespoons Dijon mustard

Salt and pepper to taste

1 cup low-sodium beef broth

1/3 cup all-purpose flour

1 cup reduced-fat sour cream

Instructions:

1. Combine the beef, onion, mushrooms, garlic and parsley in the slow cooker.
2. Stir in the mustard, salt and pepper.

3. Whisk the broth into the flour until smooth and well blended then stir in to the slow cooker.
4. Cover and cook on high heat for 1 hour then reduce to low heat and cook for another 7 to 8 hours.
5. Turn off the slow cooker and stir in the sour cream. Serve hot over noodles.

Chicken Provencal

Servings: 4 to 6

Ingredients:

2 lbs. chicken drumsticks

1 (15 ounce) can diced tomatoes

1 small yellow onion, sliced thin

1 small red pepper, sliced thin

1 (15 ounce) can white cannellini beans, rinsed and drained

1 tablespoon fresh chopped basil

2 teaspoons minced garlic

Salt and pepper to taste

Instructions:

1. Arrange the chicken drumsticks in the slow cooker.
2. Add the remaining ingredients.
3. Cover and cook on low heat for 8 hours until the chicken is cooked through.

Satsuma Turkey with Steamed Rice

Servings: 8

Ingredients:

1 large red onion, chopped

¾ cups sweet white wine

Juice from 2 large oranges

¼ cup orange marmalade

½ tablespoon tamarind paste

1 teaspoon Chinese five-spice powder

½ teaspoon red pepper flakes

1 tablespoon olive oil

2 lbs. boneless turkey breast, chopped

2 cups mandarin orange slices

1 ½ tablespoons cornstarch

Instructions:

1. Combine the red onion, white wine, orange juice, marmalade, tamarind paste, five-spice powder and red pepper flakes in the slow cooker.

2. Heat the oil in a large skillet over medium-high heat.
3. Add the turkey and cook for 5 minutes, stirring occasionally, until evenly browned.
4. Spoon the turkey into the slow cooker and top with the mandarin oranges.
5. Cover and cook on low heat for 4 hours.
6. Remove the turkey to a serving dish with a slotted spoon.
7. Pour the cooking liquid into a saucepan.
8. Spoon off ¼ cup of the cooking liquid and whisk in the cornstarch.
9. Whisk the mixture into the saucepan and bring to a boil then reduce heat and simmer for 2 minutes until thick.
10. Serve the turkey hot with the sauce.

Meatballs in Spicy, Chunky Tomato Ragu

Servings: 6

Ingredients:

¼ cup tomato paste

1 (28 ounce) can whole tomatoes, chopped

Pinch salt

½ teaspoon red pepper flakes

1 teaspoon orange zest

1 ½ lbs. lean ground beef

½ cup plain breadcrumbs

¼ cup diced yellow onion

1 large egg

½ teaspoon dried oregano

Pinch ground cinnamon

Instructions:

1. Whisk together the tomato paste, tomatoes, salt, red pepper flakes and orange zest in the slow cooker.

2. In a mixing bowl, combine the remaining ingredients.
3. Shape the meat mixture by hand into about 30 meatballs.
4. Heat the oil in a large skillet over medium-high heat.
5. Add the meatballs, half a batch at a time, and cook for 3 minutes or so, stirring often, until browned.
6. Transfer the meatballs to the slow cooker then cover and cook on low heat for 6 hours until heated through.

Chinese Beef and Noodles

Servings: 8

Ingredients:

2 lbs. boneless beef chuck roast, trimmed

¼ cup reduced-sodium soy sauce

1 ½ tablespoons hoisin sauce

1 tablespoon tomato sauce

1 teaspoon honey

1 teaspoon fresh minced ginger

1 teaspoon minced garlic

3 tablespoons rice wine vinegar

½ teaspoon dark sesame oil

16 ounces Chinese-style noodles, cooked

1 cup sliced Chinese cabbage

½ cup fresh chopped cilantro

Instructions:

1. Place the beef in the slow cooker.
2. Whisk together the soy sauce, hoisin, tomato sauce, honey, ginger, garlic, rice wine vinegar and sesame oil.
3. Pour the sauce over the beef in the slow cooker.
4. Cover and cook on low heat for 3 ½ to 4 hours until the beef is tender.
5. Remove the beef to a cutting board and let rest for 10 minutes then shred it with two forks.
6. Strain the cooking liquid through a mesh strainer and discard the solids.
7. Pour the liquid into the slow cooker and add the shredded beef.
8. Stir in the noodles, cabbage and cilantro and cook for 5 minutes on low heat.
9. Spoon into bowls and serve hot.

Tunisian-Style Lamb with Pumpkin Couscous

Servings: 6

Ingredients:

1 tablespoon olive oil

6 lamb shanks, fat trimmed

2 medium red onion, sliced thin

1 tablespoon minced garlic

1 tablespoon ground cumin

2 teaspoons ground coriander

1 ½ teaspoons paprika

1 teaspoon ground cinnamon

4 cups low-sodium beef broth

2 (15 ounce) cans diced tomatoes

2 tablespoons sugar

½ cup fresh chopped cilantro, divided

3 cups chopped pumpkin

2 cups uncooked couscous

Instructions:

1. Heat the oil in a large skillet over medium-high heat.
2. Add the lamb and cook for 2 to 3 minutes on each side until browned.
3. Combine the onion, garlic, cumin, cinnamon, coriander, and paprika in the slow cooker.
4. Stir in the beef broth, tomatoes, sugar and half the fresh cilantro.
5. Add the lamb then cover and cook for 4 hours on low heat until the lamb is cooked through.
6. Stir in the pumpkin and cook for another hour until it is tender.
7. Transfer the lamb to a serving bowl with 2 cups of the cooking liquid.
8. Stir the couscous into the slow cooker and let sit for 5 minutes until it absorbs the liquid.
9. Serve the lamb hot with the pumpkin couscous, garnished with remaining cilantro.

Rosemary Lamb Shanks

Servings: 6

Ingredients:

2 medium yellow onions, chopped

2 tablespoons olive oil

5 lbs. bone-in lamb shanks

1 cup dry red wine

2 tablespoons Dijon mustard

1 tablespoon fresh chopped rosemary

1 tablespoon minced garlic

1 teaspoon balsamic vinegar

Salt and pepper to taste

Instructions:

1. Spread the onions in the bottom of the slow cooker.
2. Heat the olive oil in a large skillet over medium-high heat.
3. Add the lamb and cook for 2 to 3 minutes on each side until lightly browned.
4. Place the lamb in the slow cooker on top of the onions.

5. Whisk together the remaining ingredients and pour into the slow cooker.
6. Cover and cook on high heat for 2 hours then reduce to low heat and cook for another 6 to 8 hours until the lamb is tender.

Chicken and Broccoli Bake

Servings: 6

Ingredients:

1 ½ cups uncooked long-grain-rice

2 lbs. boneless skinless chicken breast, chopped

1 (16 ounce) bag frozen broccoli florets

2 cups thinly sliced carrot

2 cups reduced-fat shredded cheddar cheese

1 (10.75 ounce) condensed cream of chicken soup

1 ½ cups chicken broth

Instructions:

1. Lightly grease the insert of your slow cooker.
2. Spoon the rice into the slow cooker and top with the chicken, broccoli, carrots and 1 cup cheese.
3. Pour in the soup and top with the remaining cheese.
4. Pour the broth into the slow cooker around the edges – do not stir.
5. Cover and cook on low heat for 6 hours until hot and bubbling. Serve hot.

Chicken and Chorizo Jambalaya

Servings: 8

Ingredients:

2 cups chopped yellow onion

1 cup diced celery

1 cup water

1 lbs. boneless skinless chicken breast, chopped

½ lbs. chorizo sausage, sliced

1 (14.5 ounce) can diced tomatoes

1 teaspoon Cajun seasoning

¼ teaspoon dried thyme

1 lbs. uncooked shrimp, peeled and deveined

4 cups cooked rice, hot

Instructions:

1. Combine the onion, celery, water, chicken, sausage and tomatoes in the slow cooker.
2. Stir in the Cajun seasoning and thyme.

3. Cover and cook on low heat for 6 to 7 hours.
4. Stir in the shrimp and cook on low heat for another 10 minutes or so until the shrimp is just cooked through.
5. Stir in the rice and serve hot.

Chicken Cacciatore

Servings: 8

Ingredients:

1 tablespoon olive oil

4 lbs. chicken thighs and drumsticks, skin removed

Salt and pepper to taste

8 ounces sliced mushrooms

1 large yellow onion, sliced

1 large red pepper, cored and sliced

2 tablespoons minced garlic

½ cup dry white wine

¼ cup all-purpose flour

2 teaspoons dried oregano

1 teaspoon dried thyme

1 (28 ounce) can whole tomatoes, chopped

Fresh chopped basil

Instructions:

1. Heat the oil in a large skillet over medium-high heat.
2. Season the chicken lightly with salt and pepper to taste then add to the skillet.
3. Cook for 2 to 3 minutes on each side until evenly browned then transfer to the slow cooker.
4. Add the mushrooms, onion, garlic and red pepper.
5. Stir together the wine, flour, oregano and thyme then pour it into the slow cooker with the tomatoes.
6. Cover and cook on low heat for 3 to 4 hours until the chicken is cooked through and tender.
7. Garnish with fresh basil leaves to serve.

Five-Spice Caramel Pork (Thit Heo Kho Tieu)

Servings: 8

Ingredients:

1 tablespoon olive oil

1 lbs. boneless pork belly, chopped

8 shallots, sliced thin

1 cup sliced mushrooms

1 small red pepper, sliced thin

2 teaspoons minced garlic

¼ cup reduced-sodium soy sauce

¾ cup palm sugar, finely chopped

1 cup water

2 whole star anise

1 tablespoon fish sauce

1 ¼ teaspoon Chinese five-spice powder

½ cup sliced green onion

Instructions:

1. Heat the oil in a large skillet over medium-high heat.
2. Add the pork and cook for 2 to 3 minutes on each side until lightly browned.
3. Transfer the pork to the slow cooker and stir in the shallots, mushrooms, red pepper and garlic.
4. Stir together the soy sauce, palm sugar, water, star anise, fish sauce and Chinese five-spice powder.
5. Pour the sauce into the slow cooker and stir well.
6. Cover and cook on 3 to 4 hours until the pork is cooked through.
7. Serve hot over steamed rice, garnished with sliced green onion.

Healthy Slow Cooker Recipes

Shepherd's Pie

Servings: 6

Ingredients:

2 lbs. Yukon gold potatoes, peeled and quartered

2 tablespoons butter

1/3 cup fat-free milk

Salt and pepper to taste

1 lbs. lean ground beef

1 large yellow onion, diced

1 teaspoon minced garlic

3 tablespoons tomato paste

2 cups diced mushrooms

½ cup diced carrots

1 cup low-sodium beef broth

¼ cup dry white wine

1 ½ teaspoons Worcestershire sauce

¼ cup frozen peas

cup reduced-fat shredded cheddar cheese

Instructions:

1. Place the potatoes in a large pot of salted water then bring to a boil.
2. Boil the potatoes for 12 to 15 minutes until tender then drain.
3. Mash the potatoes with the milk and butter then season with salt and pepper to taste.
4. Heat the beef, onion and garlic in a large skillet over medium heat until browned.
5. Stir in the tomato paste, mushrooms, carrots, beef broth, wine and Worcestershire sauce.
6. Simmer for 5 minutes then stir in the peas.
7. Transfer the beef mixture to the slow cooker then spread the potatoes over the top and sprinkle with cheese.
8. Cover and cook for 5 to 6 hours until hot and bubbling. Serve hot.

Meatloaf

Servings: 6

Ingredients:

2 large Yukon gold potatoes, peeled and chopped

1 lbs. lean ground beef

1 ½ lbs. lean ground turkey

1 large yellow onion, diced

½ cup ketchup

½ cup plain breadcrumbs

2 large eggs

Salt and pepper to taste

Instructions:

1. Spread the potatoes in the bottom of the slow cooker.
2. Combine the remaining ingredients in a mixing bowl until well combined.
3. Shape the mixture by hand into a loaf then place on top of the potatoes.
4. Cover and cook for 7 to 9 hours until the beef is cooked through. Serve hot.

Sweet Treat Recipes

Recipes Included in this Section:

Almond Apple Streusel

Spiced Pumpkin Pie Pudding

Walnut-Stuffed Apples

Triple Berry Cobbler

Pear Caramel Pudding

Fudgy Chocolate Cola Cake

Cinnamon Rice Pudding

Poached Pears with Balsamic Vinegar

Pineapple Bananas Foster

Tropical Coconut Tapioca Pudding

Almond Apple Streusel

Servings: 8

Ingredients:

6 cups tart apples, peeled and sliced

1 ½ teaspoons ground cinnamon

¼ teaspoon ground nutmeg

¾ cups fat-free milk

2 tablespoons melted coconut oil

½ cup granulated sugar

¼ cup honey

2 large eggs

1 ¼ teaspoons vanilla extract

½ cup plus 2 tablespoons baking mix

For the Topping:

1 cup biscuit baking mix

¼ cup light brown sugar, packed

3 tablespoons coconut oil

½ cup thinly sliced almonds

Instructions:

1. Lightly grease the insert of your slow cooker with cooking spray.
2. Place the apples in a mixing bowl and toss with the cinnamon and nutmeg to coat.
3. Transfer the apples to the slow cooker.
4. In a small bowl, whisk together the milk, coconut oil, sugar, eggs, vanilla extract and baking mix until smooth.
5. Spoon the batter over the apples in the slow cooker.
6. To prepare the topping, combine the biscuit mix and brown sugar in a mixing bowl then cut in the coconut oil until it forms a crumbled mixture.
7. Fold in the almonds then sprinkle the mixture over the apples.
8. Cover and cook on low heat for 6 to 8 hours until the apples are hot and bubbling.

Spiced Pumpkin Pie Pudding

Servings: 8

Ingredients:

1 (15 ounce) can solid-pack pumpkin

1 (12 ounce) can evaporated milk

2/3 cup granulated sugar

½ cup baking mix

2 large eggs, whisked

2 tablespoons melted coconut oil

1 ½ teaspoons ground cinnamon

½ teaspoon ground nutmeg

Pinch ground cloves

1 ½ teaspoons vanilla extract

Instructions:

1. Lightly grease the insert of your slow cooker with cooking spray.
2. Stir together the pumpkin, evaporated milk, sugar, baking mix and eggs in a mixing bowl.

3. Whisk in the melted coconut oil, cinnamon, nutmeg, cloves and vanilla extract.
4. Spread the mixture in the slow cooker then cover and cook on low heat for 6 to 7 hours until thick and hot.
5. Spoon into bowls and drizzle with light cream or top with light whipped topping to serve.

Walnut-Stuffed Apples

Servings: 6

Ingredients:

6 medium ripe apples

½ cup seedless raisins

¼ cup light brown sugar, packed

3 tablespoons finely chopped walnuts

¼ teaspoon ground cinnamon

Pinch ground nutmeg

Instructions:

1. Slice the tops off the apples and carefully remove the cores, leaving the bottom of each apple intact.
2. Stir together the raisins, brown sugar, walnuts, cinnamon and nutmeg in a mixing bowl.
3. Spoon the mixture into the apples and place them in the slow cooker.
4. Cover and cook on low heat for 4 to 5 hours until the apples are tender.

Triple Berry Cobbler

Servings: 8

Ingredients:

1 ¼ cups all-purpose flour, divided

1 cup plus 2 tablespoons granulated sugar, divided

1 teaspoon baking powder

1/8 teaspoon ground cinnamon

1 large egg, whisked

¼ cup skim milk

2 tablespoons coconut oil, melted

1 cup fresh sliced strawberries

½ cup fresh blueberries

½ cup fresh raspberries

Pinch salt

Instructions:

1. Lightly grease the insert of your slow cooker with cooking spray.
2. Whisk together 1 cup of flour, 2 tablespoons sugar, baking powder and cinnamon in a mixing bowl.

3. In a separate bowl, whisk together the egg, milk and coconut oil.
4. Stir the wet ingredients into the dry until just combined then spread in the slow cooker.
5. Combine the remaining ¼ cup flour with the salt and remaining 1 cup sugar in a mixing bowl.
6. Toss with the berries then sprinkle into the slow cooker.
7. Cover and cook on high heat for 2 to 2 ½ hours until hot and bubbling.

Peach Caramel Pudding

Servings: 8 to 10

Ingredients:

1 cup all-purpose flour

½ cup granulated sugar

1 ¼ teaspoons baking powder

¾ teaspoon ground cinnamon

¼ teaspoon salt

½ cup 1% milk

4 large ripe peaches, pitted and sliced

½ cup chopped pecans

¾ cup light brown sugar, packed

¼ cup melted coconut oil

½ cup boiling water

Instructions:

1. Lightly grease the insert of your slow cooker with cooking spray.
2. Whisk together the flour, sugar, baking powder, cinnamon and salt in a mixing bowl. Stir in the milk.

3. Toss in the peaches and pecans to coat then spread in the slow cooker.
4. Whisk together the brown sugar and coconut oil in another bowl.
5. Whisk in the boiling water then pour over the ingredients in the slow cooker – do not stir.
6. Cover and cook on low heat for 3 to 4 hours until the peaches are tender and bubbling.
7. Serve the pudding warm in dessert bowls drizzled with milk or light cream, if desired.

Fudgy Chocolate Cola Cake

Servings: 8

Ingredients:

1 ½ cups all-purpose flour

½ cup granulated sugar

¼ cup semisweet chocolate chips

2 ¼ teaspoons baking powder

¼ teaspoon salt

1 cup reduced-fat chocolate milk

½ cup coconut oil, melted

1 ½ teaspoons vanilla extract

½ cup canned diet cola

Instructions:

1. Lightly grease the insert of your slow cooker with cooking spray.
2. Whisk together the flour, sugar, chocolate chips, baking powder and salt in a mixing bowl.
3. In a separate bowl, whisk together the chocolate milk, coconut oil and vanilla extract.

Fudgy Chocolate Cola Cake

4. Stir the wet ingredients into the dry until smooth and combined then whisk in the cola.
5. Pour the mixture into the slow cooker then cover and cook on high heat for 2 to 2 ½ hours or until the cake is set.
6. Turn off heat and let stand for 30 minutes.
7. Spoon into dessert cups to serve.

Cinnamon Rice Pudding

Servings: 4

Ingredients:

1 ¼ cups 1% milk

½ cup granulated sugar

½ cup uncooked rice

1/3 cup seedless raisins

2 large eggs, whisked

1 ¼ teaspoons ground cinnamon

1 ½ teaspoons melted coconut oil

1 teaspoon vanilla extract

Instructions:

1. Stir together the milk, sugar, rice, raisins, eggs and cinnamon in the slow cooker.
2. Whisk in the coconut oil and vanilla extract until smooth.
3. Cover and cook on low heat for 2 hours then stir and cook for another 1 to 2 hours until the rice is tender.
4. Spoon into bowls and chill until ready to serve.

Poached Pears with Balsamic Vinegar

Servings: 8

Ingredients:

1 ½ cups cranberry juice (unsweetened)

¼ cup light brown sugar, packed

2 tablespoons dried cherries, chopped

3 teaspoons ground cinnamon

4 large ripe pears

Balsamic vinegar to taste

Instructions:

1. Lightly grease the insert of your slow cooker with cooking spray.
2. Stir together the cranberry juice, brown sugar, cherries and cinnamon in the slow cooker.
3. Carefully peel the pears and cut them in half lengthwise before adding them to the slow cooker.
4. Cover and cook on low heat for 4 to 5 hours until the pears are tender.
5. Serve the pears warm in bowls, drizzled with balsamic vinegar.

Pineapple Bananas Foster

Servings: 8

Ingredients:

½ cup brown sugar, packed

3 tablespoons coconut oil

¼ cup light coconut milk

¼ cup dark rum

1 ½ cups canned pineapple, drained

4 medium ripe bananas, peeled and sliced

½ teaspoon ground cinnamon

Instructions:

1. Lightly grease the insert of your slow cooker with cooking spray.
2. Stir together the brown sugar, coconut oil, coconut milk and rum in the slow cooker, stirring until well combined.
3. Cover and cook on low heat for 1 hour then stir smooth.
4. Stir in the pineapple, banana and cinnamon.
5. Cover and cook on low heat for another 15 minutes then serve hot.

Tropical Coconut Tapioca Pudding

Servings: 8

Ingredients:

¾ cup granulated sugar

½ cup small pearl tapioca, uncooked

2 (14 ounce) cans light coconut milk

1 large egg

¾ cup fresh pineapple, diced

½ cup shredded unsweetened coconut

Instructions:

1. Lightly grease the insert of your slow cooker with cooking spray.
2. Whisk together the sugar, tapioca pearls and coconut milk in a mixing bowl then pour into the slow cooker.
3. Cover and cook the tapioca on low heat for 2 hours.
4. Beat the egg in a small mixing bowl then whisk in ½ cup of the cooked tapioca.
5. Pour the egg mixture into the slow cooker and whisk to incorporate.
6. Cover and cook on low heat for another 30 minutes then turn off the slow cooker.

7. Stir in the pineapple then cover and let rest for 30 minutes before serving.
8. Sprinkle with shredded coconut to garnish.

Conclusion

After reading this book you should have a good understanding of what slow cooking is and how it can benefit your family. Rather than spending an hour or more after work every day just to put a healthy meal on the table you can throw a recipe together in the morning and return home from work to find a hot meal waiting to be enjoyed. If you are serious about improving and maintaining your health, slow cooking is definitely the way to go. Try out some of the recipes in this book for yourself to see just how great slow cooking can be!

Happy Eating,

Sophie

About the Author

Best-selling Author Sophie Miller is a long-time lover of food and cooking. Her first memory of cooking is making Bolognese with her mother, and scones and brown bread with her grandmother. She has worked as a chef in numerous restaurants and ran her own café which concentrated on healthy eating. She loves going to farmers markets with her produce and sharing stories and recipes with other stall owners. She has ten publications to her name so far and is currently working on more exciting cookbooks.

Sophie eats a mostly wheat-free diet, the bloated stomach was not a good look for her! She loves veggies from her own vegetable patch and she really enjoys to cook and bake vegan goods for her best friend. Her husband eats everything (apart from cucumber) so she cooks a range of different food to keep the entire household happy.

Sophie lives in the country with her husband, six dogs, two horses, 11 ducks and soon to be chickens! Friends call her the most organised person they know and love going to dinner parties in her house. Family Christmas dinner is traditionally ALWAYS in Sophie's abode and family travel from far and wide to celebrate the day there, enjoying a spectacular five course meal... She loves travelling and experimenting with dishes she has tasted while abroad when she gets back.

Grab one of her Sophie's other books below, you won't be disappointed....

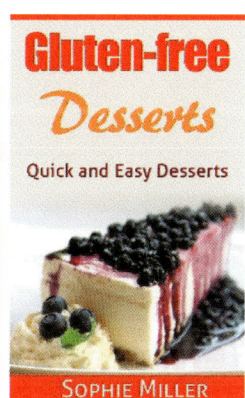

5:2
VEGAN
DIET
RECIPES
Your complete guide to how and why the fast diet works
SOPHIE MILLER

Gluten-free
MEDITERRANEAN
DIET COOKBOOK
25 Delicious Recipes from the healthiest region in the world!
SOPHIE MILLER

GLUTEN-FREE
DESSERTS
UNDER 200
CALORIES
SOPHIE MILLER

GLUTEN-FREE
VEGAN
COOKBOOK
Quick and Easy Recipes to aid Weightloss
SOPHIE MILLER

Gluten-free
VEGAN SLOW
COOKER
Quick and easy recipes for busy people
SOPHIE MILLER

Printed in Great Britain
by Amazon